LAW OFFICE ON A LAPTOP

HOW TO SET UP YOUR OWN SUCCESSFUL MOBILE LAW PRACTICE

Second Edition

By: Catherine Hodder, Esq. &

Kelly C. Sturmthal, Esq.

www.gosoloforsuccess.com

Copyright © Catherine Hodder, Esq. and Kelly C. Sturmthal, Esq. 2017. All rights reserved.

No part of this publication may be reproduced, stored in a retrieval system or transmitted in any form or by any means without the prior written permission of the authors except in accordance with the provisions of the Copyright, Designs and Patents Act of 1988.

This book is not intended to provide personalized legal, tax, business, or financial advice. The authors specifically disclaim any liability, loss or risk, personal or otherwise, that is incurred as a consequence, directly or indirectly, of the use and application of any of the contents of this book.

Energy and persistence conquer all things

– Benjamin Franklin

TABLE OF CONTENTS

Introduction	8
Chapter 1. Getting Started	17
Identify Your Specialty	18
Check State Requirements	20
Make a Business Plan	24
Calculate Overhead	27
Check Your Gut Instincts	30
Chapter 2. Setting Up Practice	33
Determine Corporate Structure	34
Apply for Taxpayer Id Number	37
Obtain Business License(s)	37
Assemble Support Team	38
Set Up Bank & Escrow Accounts	40
Set Up Merchant Accounts	42
Investigate Liability Insurance	45

Chapter 3. Setting Up Procedures   49

    Create Intake Form   50

    Set Up a Database   51

    Create New Client Checklist   53

    Develop a Conflicts Check   54

    Determine Fee Structure   56

    Draft Retainer/Fee Agreement   58

    Draft Collection Letters   61

    Thank Referral Sources   64

    Draft Closing Letter   65

    Get Forms & Resources   66

    State by State Resource Guide   68

Chapter 4. Setting Up Systems   79

    Find Accounting Software   80

    Compare Management Programs   81

    Set Up a Voice Mail Account   83

    Find Legal Research Resources   84

    Set Up Document Preparation   85

    Retain and Back Up Files   86

Chapter 5. Marketing & Getting Clients — 89

- Know Your Bar Rules — 90
- Craft Your "Elevator Speech" — 93
- Create a Standout Business Card — 94
- Design a Professional Website — 96
- Advertise Your Website — 99
- Blog on Your Area of Expertise — 102
- Embrace Social Media — 105
- Seek Out Live Presentations — 114
- Develop Strategic Partners — 116
- Join Networking Groups — 117
- Create a Networking Group — 118
- Write Articles — 121
- Write a Newsletter — 122

Chapter 6. Other Considerations — 125

- Do You Want a Partner? — 125
- Who is Your Backup? — 128
- Three Rules for a Mobile Law Practice — 129
- Ten Tips for a Successful Practice — 131
- How Do You Quantify Success? — 136

WHY A SECOND EDITION?

When we wrote *Law Office on a Laptop* almost two years ago, our goal was to introduce how to embrace and utilize technology to create and enhance a mobile law practice. Since then, there have been numerous advancements in technology, greater acceptance of the mobile law practice concept, and a growing amount of resources available to market and manage your mobile law practice.

Social media has continued to grow and become a viable way to promote your firm while networking. We have expanded the information on marketing and social media to explain Facebook, LinkedIn, Twitter, Instagram, and YouTube.

INTRODUCTION

Do you remember the day you passed the bar exam? It took a lot of work to get there, and the feeling of accomplishment after passing was HUGE. The next big hurdle was to find an ideal job, but for many of us, we had to pursue an area of law where we could get a job. Was that the right fit for you?

Are you where you want to be in your career? Are you tired of working for a large firm with no control over your hours? Did you take a break from law? Did you postpone your legal career to start a family or take care of a loved one? Did you just graduate and realize that law school did not teach you how to start or manage a law practice? Regardless of your path, you chose this book to take the next step. So, here we go...

We created this book from a desire to use our experiences of starting our own mobile law office to educate others who wish to have more control over their careers. Although we have tailored this for those in the legal profession, consultants or other entrepreneurs who are interested in the mobile office concept could easily adapt these concepts to use as a blueprint.

WHAT IS A MOBILE LAW OFFICE?

Essentially, a law practice designed to be available whenever your clients need you. You can satisfy those needs without having to travel to a brick and mortar practice. Because of technology, many professionals can run their businesses from their laptops, notebooks, iPads, and smartphones. We embarked on a mission to figure out if we, as lawyers, could also create a practice that was completely mobile. We wanted to control our time, control our overhead, and control our office systems. After some good planning and lots of decisions, we made it happen! Sharing the blueprint was always part of our plan. We know there are many talented lawyers that can make this structure work for their lives and their family. Structuring your practice as a mobile law office allows you the flexibility to meet your clients, to work from your home office or to move between different offices. When you structure your *Law Office on a Laptop*, you have control over your hours, your overhead, and your life.

GOALS + OPPORTUNITIES = SUCCESS

Throughout this book, we will provide a practical checklist of GOALS for you to accomplish and OPPORTUNITIES to pursue. By the end of your journey within this book, you will have a concrete plan of action to start your own business. Most of this may seem to be common sense, but we have successfully tried each of these items on the checklists and proven that a mobile law office is a viable option. Of course, we have uncovered a few nuggets of wisdom along the way and we will be sharing those as well. At the end of each chapter, look for the goals for you to achieve and the opportunities to go after to help you be more successful. These actionable items will keep you on track by efficiently and effectively providing you with the blueprint to start your own law firm.

SAMPLE FORMS & LINKS

This book is intended to help you, encourage you, and most importantly, **to save you time!** We have provided sample forms, direct links, and website addresses to state bar associations, businesses, and vendors that may give you more information or help your practice succeed.

SUPPORT AND RESOURCES

In addition to the information and resources in this book, we provide on-going encouragement and support for your practice.

Read our Blog: **www.GoSoloForSuccess.com**

"Like" us on Facebook at **GoSoloForSuccess**

Follow us on Twitter at **@GoSolo4Success**

Follow us on Instagram at **GoSolo4Success**

Follow us on Pinterest at **GoSoloForSuccess**

You will find practical wisdom and support as you take this journey of starting your own mobile law office.

OUR STORY

Kelly and I met through our local MOM's club and we found common ground as attorneys and having taken time off from our careers when our kids were young. At that time, Kelly was working part time for a law firm and I was considering going back into the workforce. I asked her: "How did you do it? Balancing a legal career and family life?"

And she honestly replied with, "I didn't!" The sad reality is that working "part time" at a law firm is really "full time" in any other profession. Like me, she was looking for an alternative to be able to practice law but still have control over the amount of time she put in at the office while remaining available for her children.

We also had common life experiences. My father had a ten-year battle with Alzheimer's disease and Kelly's father died from an aggressive cancer. From personal experiences, we understood how important estate planning could be to help families. We knew first-hand how having the right documents in place -- Durable Power of Attorney, Health Care Surrogate, Living Will, Last Will and Testament, and Trust -- made huge differences in how our fathers' affairs were handled. We also knew that most people don't understand these important aspects of their loved one's estates until they are faced with it themselves.

In law school, we were taught about estate planning in a generic manner, but it is different to experience it personally. We wanted to educate others from our experiences and help them navigate through difficult life events like disability and death.

Also, we found that estate planning law firms were largely courting clients with high net worth. Due to the overhead involved, it was not profitable for the firms to make basic estate planning affordable for young families with few assets. We thought it was important to focus our practice on reaching the underserved and overlooked clients. We wanted to reach families with young children who really were most concerned with guardianship of their children rather than saving on estate taxes.

Since we would serve the needs of young families, we instantly recognized that we would have to be flexible. To meet with an attorney, our clients would have to hire a babysitter or take time off work. With busy work and school schedules, even having a husband and wife agree on a meeting time was a challenge. We created our business model on adapting to their schedules. We began to meet clients at their home or office thus eliminating the need for a babysitter or a client having to leave work.

We also set out to work with small businesses and entrepreneurs. These are extremely busy individuals and they appreciated our flexibility that involved meeting them at their place of business. They also generally preferred to communicate through email, text, phone and fax. We did not have to be tied down to a stationary office. Technology made all of it possible.

In designing our practice to meet the needs of our clients, we created and adapted to the mobile law office concept. As with any business endeavor, we had to look at the benefits and challenges of this business model.

The benefits were:

- Control over our hours
- Control over the clients we wanted
- Control over our overhead
- Control to make the money we wanted

The challenges were:

- Administrative work of running our own business
- Client acceptance of a mobile law office

We wondered if we would be taken seriously. With the help of technology, we discovered that the administrative aspects of our business could be streamlined. With the latest online services and computer software, we could manage our law practice. Pleasantly surprised by how much our clients appreciated our business model, we found that clients did not necessarily care to meet in an oak paneled boardroom with imposing law tomes that no one reads. Clients soon realized that the fancier office, the higher the fees they might have to pay.

Our business soon took off. We were on to something. Many attorneys that we met loved our "mobile law office" concept and wanted to know how they could do it. Our clients were happy with our personalized service, and they recommended us to others. Most importantly, we could work the hours we wanted to and have more control over our lives. The flexibility to handle as much work as we wanted allowed us to grow the business to the extent that it fit into our lives, allowing us to balance our work and our life without sacrificing the quality of either. Of course, we also enjoyed the perks of being "mobile." For instance, if we met a client at their place of business, they might introduce us to other potential clients or pass our name along to others.

CHAPTER 1

GETTING STARTED

Is a mobile law practice right for you? It is not for everyone. While you do enjoy flexibility and control over your hours, you still must put a lot of work into it to become successful.

You should first identify your legal specialty. You must check the legal and ethical requirements in your jurisdiction. Then you should draft a business plan and calculate your overhead requirements. Finally, you must have a gut check: Does running your own firm fit your stamina and temperament?

IDENTIFY YOUR SPECIALTY

More than half the battle in being successful is enjoying the law you practice. You may have started out in a field of law where you could easily obtain a job, but as your own boss, what would you really like to do?

- **Inventory Your Skills.** Take a moment and write down all the skills and experience that you have at this point. For example: research, writing, time management, attention to detail, administrative skills, business skills, marketing, persuasiveness, advocacy, debate, etc. What is your background and experience? How can it help you in your ideal practice?

- **Find Your Passion.** Now that you know your skills, which ones do you enjoy? Do you like arguing in court or drafting contracts? Do you prefer defending people or advocating positions?

What is the law you would like to practice? Do you like researching zoning laws or helping victims of securities fraud? Do you enjoy inventions and working with entrepreneurs on patents, trademarks, and copyrights?

What is your passion? Although both of us started out in banking and contract law, our personal experiences drew us toward using our skill sets in the practice of estate planning and business planning. If you have ever been to one of our seminars, you will see our passion of educating people on how and why estate planning documents are important. For example, Catherine was never as energized about filing UCC-1 statements for collateral as she is about making sure people understood what a Living Will does and does not do.

- **Apply Skills to Your Passion.** Do your skills meet your passion? Determine not only your current experience, but also what you ultimately want to do. Contemplate how your skill set translates to this and what education or CLE courses will help you achieve those goals. Consider reaching out to attorneys who are practicing the area of law you're interested in, and ask them to evaluate your strengths.

They could potentially become a mentor to you.

- **Determine if Your Specialty Lends Itself to a Mobile Office Concept.** Does your specialty lend itself to a mobile law office concept? Can you meet with a client at his or her home or office? Can you make strategic partners to share office space or conference rooms? How can you maintain professionalism and protect client confidentiality?

CHECK STATE REQUIREMENTS

The State Bar Association will specify all the requirements and ethical guidelines for your practice. Do you need to maintain an escrow account? Is there a requirement for mandatory professional liability insurance? What are the rules of advertising in your jurisdiction?

We have listed all the Bar Associations in the 50 states with links to their websites. Most of these websites are tremendously helpful in giving guidance for new law firms and solo attorneys. Review the Rules of Professional Conduct for your state.

STATE BAR ASSOCIATION WEBSITES

ALABAMA	www.alabar.org
ALASKA	www.alaskabar.org
ARIZONA	www.azbar.org
ARKANSAS	www.arkbar.org
CALIFORNIA	www.calbar.ca.gov
COLORADO	www.cobar.org
CONNECTICUT	www.ctbar.org
DELAWARE	www.dsba.org
D.C.	www.dcbar.org
FLORIDA	www.floridabar.org
GEORGIA	www.gabar.org
HAWAII	www.hsba.org
IDAHO	www.isb.idaho.gov
INDIANA	www.indybar.org
IOWA	www.iowabar.org
KANSAS	www.ksbar.org

KENTUCKY	www.kybar.org
LOUISIANA	www.lsba.org
MAINE	www.mainebar.org
MARYLAND	www.msba.org
MASSACHUSETTS	www.massbar.org
MICHIGAN	www.michbar.org
MINNESOTA	www.mnbar.org
MISSISSIPPI	www.msbar.org
MISSOURI	www.mobar.org
MONTANA	www.montanabar.org
NEBRASKA	www.nebar.com
NEVADA	www.nvbar.org
NEW HAMPSHIRE	www.nhbar.org
NEW JERSEY	www.njsba.com
NEW MEXICO	www.nmbar.org
NEW YORK	www.nysba.org
NORTH CAROLINA	www.ncbar.org
NORTH DAKOTA	www.sband.org
OHIO	www.ohiobar.org

OKLAHOMA	www.okbar.org
OREGON	www.osbar.org
PENNSYLVANIA	www.pabar.org
RHODE ISLAND	www.ribar.com
SOUTH CAROLINA	www.scbar.org
SOUTH DAKOTA	www.sdbar.org
TENNESSEE	www.tba.org
TEXAS	www.texasbar.com
UTAH	www.utahbar.org
VERMONT	www.vtbar.org
VIRGINIA	www.vba.org
WASHINGTON	www.wsba.org
WEST VIRGINIA	www.wvbar.org
WISCONSIN	www.wisbar.org
WYOMING	www.wyomingbar.org

MAKE A BUSINESS PLAN

You went to law school not business school. But if you want to be a solo practitioner, you must think like an entrepreneur. Going through the exercise of writing a business plan will help you to focus on your talents, strengths, weaknesses, and identify where you may need help.

Most solo practitioners start small and self-finance their startup costs. However, if you were to ask a bank for a loan, they would want to see your business plan as part of the application process.

Your business plan does not need to be formal, but it should be organized. There are many books and online resources for writing a business plan. The US Small Business Association (SBA) is a great resource for developing your business plan. Learn more at **www.sba.gov**.

You can also contact SCORE which is supported by the U.S. Small Business Administration. SCORE provides tools, webinars, workshops, and mentors for your business. You can find your local SCORE office at **www.score.org**.

ELEMENTS OF A BUSINESS PLAN

- **Executive Summary** – A brief statement of what you want out of this plan.

- **Business Description** – What is the area of law you will be practicing?

- **Target Market** – Who do you want to serve? Are you looking for corporate clients? Older individuals who may need help with Medicare or elder care? People going through divorce?

- **Competitive Analysis** – In your community, who else is practicing law in your area of expertise? What talents or strategy do you have that sets you apart from your competition?

- **Marketing Plan** – Once you have identified your market, how are you going to reach them? How will you get your message to your audience? If you want to reach business owners, consider joining local business networking groups or trade associations. If you want to reach younger populations, advertise at schools. If you want to target your services to older populations, consider advertising in church bulletins. A good resource is *The One Page Marketing Plan* by Allan Dib.

- **Operations & Management** – Outline your organization. If you have a partner or assistant, who is responsible for what? What computer systems, software, and online resources will you need to effectively manage your practice?

- **Financial Plan** – Are you self-financing or getting a loan? Do you need money for upfront costs? What do you need to invest now and what expenses can you pay later? And the most important question: What is your overhead expense?

CALCULATE OVERHEAD

Part of making a business plan is calculating and understanding the expenses you will incur. Determine what your "one time" expenses are and your ongoing monthly expenses.

Evaluate every system and every monthly charge to make sure you know how much you must make each month to cover your overhead. It is very easy for overhead to accumulate, but it is hard to reduce.

For each expense, ask yourself if the overhead you are taking on is truly the most efficient and cost effective. Review your business plan with your accountant or a friend who has their own business or law firm. They may point out areas that you need to consider.

In calculating overhead, look at both the large and small, one-time and on-going expenses in running your firm. Consider your options for telephone, computers, mobile phones, legal research, document-drafting programs, and accounting software. Considering today's technology, do you need a landline if you are going to have your mobile phone with you everywhere? We will go into depth later with recommendations for low cost ways to manage your practice. Just take the time to research each fixed or recurring expense to see if it is the most cost-effective.

The largest expense you will face is office space. In starting our practice, we did not want to be bound by huge overhead. We realized that our clients did not mind that we did not have a fancy office with the huge boardroom. They appreciated the convenience of our "house calls." In fact, we found that clients were more relaxed in their own settings.

We formed networks with attorneys and business professionals. Many offered us use of their empty boardrooms and office spaces when we needed it. When our practice became very busy, we rented a shared office suite. This was helpful when we had to witness and notarize many estate planning documents in one day as there were additional witnesses available. We also shared an assistant who greeted our clients, received incoming mail and scheduled the use of the conference room. But still, the suite rental was a mere fraction of the expense of having our own office.

Consider the expense of maintaining an office. Could the work you do be done in your home office? Could you make use of a shared office suite? Perhaps attorneys in your area have empty offices in their firms and would enjoy subletting to you? Think outside the traditional paradigm of the law office. Clients may be more comfortable talking to you in a coffee shop rather than a large wood-paneled boardroom. It is important, however to remain mindful of confidentiality and professionalism. Discussing private matters in a coffee shop may not be prudent. Also consider the convenience and benefits for your client if you make the trip to meet them. A busy entrepreneur may be grateful if you came to them during their business hours to review a contract. A family with young children may appreciate you bringing their estate planning documents to their home so the family does not have to arrange for a babysitter. Providing personalized service endears you to your client and may help to generate referrals.

Another large expense is technology. Although we advocate operating with low overhead, this is the one area that you should invest in. As a mobile law office, your success depends on having your computers, printers, scanners and office devices working well and delivering professional output. Spending more money for a quality laser printer, scanner, and copier may save you time and money if it is less susceptible to break downs or jams. We realized that efficiently processing paperwork with quality hardware and technology reduced time, money, and effort in the long run.

CHECK YOUR GUT INSTINCTS

The final step is to see if starting and running a law practice is right for you. Ask yourself the following:

- Do you have the stamina and temperament to run a practice and obtain your own clients?

- How much money do you need to make to survive and feel you are successful?

- Can you market yourself? Are you comfortable networking and putting yourself out there?

- Can you bill clients and make collections calls if delinquent?

If you can complete GOALS and go after OPPORTUNITIES, then you are well on your way.

CHAPTER 1 - GETTING STARTED

GOALS & OPPORTUNITIES CHECKLIST

Remember: Goals + Opportunities = Success

GOALS

__ *Identify Your Specialty*

__ *Inventory Your Skills*

__ *Find Your Passion*

__ *Apply Your Skills to Your Passion*

__ *Does it Work as a Mobile Law Office?*

__ *Check State Requirements*

__ *Make a Business Plan*

__ *Calculate Overhead*

__ *Check Your Gut Instincts*

OPPORTUNITIES

_ *When drafting your business plan, have others review your plan and challenge you on your business. Ask a marketing person to look at your marketing plan. Consult with a banker, accountant or financial advisor and ask them to review your numbers. Also ask a solo practitioner to go over your plan with you; he or she may give you valuable advice from their experiences.*

_ *When planning overhead expenses, reach out to other attorneys in the area to see if they have an unused office that you could sublet. Some attorneys might allow you to borrow their conference rooms on occasion. Talking to more professionals about the law you practice is more advertising for you.*

_ *When evaluating your technology needs, tell your computer experts about the services you provide. They will potentially encounter many other clients who might need your services.*

"EVERY ACCOMPLISHMENT STARTS WITH A DECISION TO TRY" – ANONYMOUS

CHAPTER 2

SETTING UP PRACTICE

To avoid problems down the road, it is important to take the time to properly set up your practice. Any planning now will benefit you in the future. Talk to as many solo practitioners as you can to get their advice or suggestions; learn what has worked for them or what they might have done differently. Most attorneys are happy to share their mistakes, war stories, and successes.

DETERMINE CORPORATE STRUCTURE

It is important to set up the proper corporate structure for your practice. Do you want to be a Professional Association or LLC or another corporate entity? There are a variety of factors that will guide you to the best choice for your situation. Important factors in corporate entity selection are protection from personal liability and tax considerations.

Will you be on your own or have a partner? Will you have employees? How do you avoid double taxation? This is where you need an expert. Find a qualified accountant, CPA or corporate tax attorney who can help you choose the right structure for you based on your situation. Make sure you check with your State Bar Association first to see if there are any specific corporate entities you may or may not form for your practice. The various entities you might consider are:

- **Professional Corporation or Professional Association.** This is a separate entity formed by filing Articles of Incorporation with the State Division of Corporations to provide legal or medical services. All shareholders are shielded from personal liability of the activities of the corporation or association; however, it is important to note that, as a lawyer, you are always subject to malpractice claims for your actions. As a corporation, there are formalities such as having shareholders, directors, adopting bylaws, keeping minutes, etc. There is generally an annual fee or franchise tax paid to the State Division of Corporations for this entity. Additionally, you may be subject to double taxation on corporate income. However, this can be resolved by filing an S Corporation Status Election with the Internal Revenue Service, whereby you can elect to pass through corporate income or losses to the respective shareholders' personal tax returns for federal income tax purposes. The election form is IRS Form 2553, Election by a Small Business Corporation.

- **Limited Liability Company (LLC) or Professional Limited Liability Company (PLLC)**: This entity has gained popularity for its flexibility in protecting small business owners from general liability but also providing for "pass-through" taxation. This is a separate entity formed by filing Articles of Organization with the State Division of Corporations. Each member is taxed on their share of profits or losses. As with Professional Corporations or Associations, each member lawyer is liable for their own malpractice. If you have more than one member in the LLC, it is recommended to draft an Operating Agreement that outlines each member's interest and responsibilities. The PLLC is for a specific service, such as the practice of law. Again, since this is a corporate entity, there will be an annual fee or franchise tax paid to the State Division of Corporations.

- **Sole Proprietorship:** This is not a separate entity filed with the State Division of Corporations, and as such there are no annual fees. This is not recommended however since there is no protection from personal liability. Essentially a sole proprietorship is an attorney doing business as himself or herself, which means their personal assets are exposed to creditors. All profits and/or losses appear on the attorney's personal tax filing.

APPLY FOR A TAXPAYER ID NUMBER

An EIN (Employee Identification Number), also called a TIN (Taxpayer Identification Number), must be obtained for your corporate entity. This number will be used in filing taxes for your entity and to set up bank accounts for your firm. It is easy to get a number by completing IRS Form SS-4 or by going to www.irs.gov and filling out an online form. You may be able to get an identification number instantly online or in a couple of days by mail.

OBTAIN BUSINESS LICENSE(S)

Contact your local county and municipal occupational or business license division or tax department. They will direct you how to register your firm and what applications must be completed. If you plan to work from home, there may be home occupational licenses that are required. Some jurisdictions require a business license for each attorney in the practice as well as a business license for the law office.

It is important to note that some jurisdictions require all legal advertisements and written communications disclose an office location. If you are truly mobile and working out of your residence, you may need to publish that address. Check with your state bar association for what the bar rules require.

ASSEMBLE SUPPORT TEAM

You need to have a team of professionals to consult when forming and running your business. They should be people from which you are comfortable with seeking advice. As they understand your practice, they may also help you find leads and be a referral source for you. Your team should be composed of:

- A trusted **CPA or Accountant** who understands small business, specifically a solo law practice.

- An **Insurance Agent** for Professional Liability Insurance. Some states do not require Professional Liability Insurance. Talk to an insurance professional to determine what is best for your situation.

- **Lawyers in your practice area** to consult with on issues that may arise in your practice. They could provide backup if you are temporarily unable to practice due to illness or extended vacations. You could also consult with them on matters that are out of your area of expertise. As you launch your practice, you might contact those attorneys and ask to handle matters or clients that might be too small for them, but they can give you more experience in the field.

- **Lawyers outside your field and professionals in your community** to discuss business matters and to refer business to one another. As your business faces challenges, you can benefit by getting ideas on what works for them. If you specialize in divorce and family law, you may want to associate yourself with an estate planning attorney who can be a resource when your clients need new estate planning documents. You should also try to network with accountants, bankers, financial planners, insurance agents, real estate agents and other professionals in your community for free advice as well as for referrals. Your clients will appreciate sound recommendations from you. In return, these professionals you associate with will refer you to their clients.

While it is helpful to have a team of professionals to support your practice, you can also network with other business owners to learn how they have become successful. Many small businesses share the same challenges as a solo law practice. If possible, consider meeting with these contacts monthly to build a rapport and a support system. Potentially, this group will be a consistent referral source in the future.

SET UP BANK & ESCROW ACCOUNTS

Go to your local bank to set up your banking accounts. The bank will need to have your entity or corporate name, the entity's Tax Identification Number, and certain corporate documents, such as Articles of Incorporation or, if an LLC, your Articles of Organization.

You need to set up at least two bank accounts for your practice: (1) for your day-to-day operating expenses; and (2) an escrow account, called an IOLTA (Interest on Law Firm Trust Account) or IOTA (Interest on Trust Accounts). If you plan to take retainers or hold funds that are unearned, you must place those funds in an escrow account. You may have more than one client's retainer in the escrow account but it is important to account for every transaction and only move funds out of escrow if the retainer is earned. Many lawyers unintentionally run afoul of bar rules from mismanagement of escrow funds. Familiarize yourself with your state bar's ethical guidelines and follow them to the letter! Most banks are well versed in setting up these types of accounts. The interest earned on the escrow account will go to your state bar association for legal aid or charitable purposes. You may also consider setting up a third account to put money into each month to save up for large expense items such as your annual professional liability insurance.

SET UP MERCHANT ACCOUNTS

Merchant accounts are set up to handle credit card transactions. If you are considering accepting credit card payments, there are many easy and low cost options. There are apps that allow you to enter a client's credit card information on your smart phone or merchant services that will give you a device so you can swipe your client's credit card. Make sure the merchant services account is linked only through your operating account, as the credit card company will have permission to take money out of your account (e.g. if a client disputes a charge). Do not let credit card companies have access to your IOTA or IOLTA escrow account.

Also, consider if you want to accept credit cards. While this is an easy way for your clients to pay, you will have to pay the merchant services company a transaction fee and perhaps a monthly fee. Compare different plans. Understand the total costs of the merchant services as the fees generally go down based on the volume of transactions. If you have few transactions, you might choose a lower monthly fee with a higher percentage per transaction fee. You should also check with your bank to see what options they provide.

MERCHANT ACCOUNT PROVIDERS

Abacus Payment   www.abacusnext.com

Go Payment   www.intuit-gopayment.com

LawPay   www.lawpay.com

PayAnywhere   www.payanywhere.com

Payline   www.paylinedata.com

PayPal   www.paypal.com

SparkPay   www.getsparkpay.com

Square   www.squareup.com

Another note about accepting credit cards: with the latest apps and systems, a signature may not be required.

If you are not having the client swipe their card or having them sign on the keypad, you may want to get written authorization to process the transaction.

For example, if you have invoiced a client and they would like to pay by credit card, you could email the sample form on the following page for them to complete and return to you.

ONE TIME CREDIT CARD PAYMENT AUTHORIZATION FORM

Please sign and complete this form to authorize [FIRM NAME] to make a one-time charge to your credit card listed below. By signing this form, you give us permission to charge your account for the amount indicated. This is permission for a single transaction only, and does not provide authorization for any additional unrelated debits or credits to your account.

Please complete the information below:

I hereby authorize [FIRM NAME] to charge my credit card in the amount indicated below. This payment is for legal services.

Client Name: _____

Billing Address: _____

Phone#: _____

Card: Visa   MasterCard   Discover

Card Number _____

Exp. Date   _____

CVV2 (3-digit number on back of Visa/MC, 4 digits on front of AMEX) _____

I authorize the above-named business to charge the credit card indicated in this authorization form according to the terms outlined above. This payment authorization is for the goods/services described above, for the amount indicated above only, and is valid for one time use only. I certify that I am an authorized user of this credit card and that I will not dispute the payment with my credit card company; so long as the transaction corresponds to the terms indicated in this form.

Client Signature

_____ Date _____

INVESTIGATE LIABILITY INSURANCE

Not all states require attorneys to carry professional liability insurance. Some jurisdictions allow a lawyer to forgo liability insurance, but they must advise a client and get a client's written acknowledgement that they have been so advised. Know what your state mandates.

If it is not required for your practice by your jurisdiction, it still may be wise to get insurance for peace of mind.

Be aware that some referral sources, such as Legal Service Plan companies, require that the attorneys they contract with have a minimum of $100,000 per claim and $300,000 overall of Professional Liability Insurance. As a solo practitioner, an annual policy could run anywhere from $1,500 to $3,000. Check with your State Bar Association and attorney friends for recommendations for insurance carriers.

"Prior Acts" coverage covers claims arising from legal services rendered before the start date of the policy. "Retroactive Date" is the date after which claims may be covered by the policy.

The factors that could impact your premium include your jurisdiction, attorney record and practice area. According to *The Washington Times*, in 2012, the most malpractice claims were in the real estate and the personal injury fields of law. As with most insurance plans, the rates depend on the deductible you are willing to pay, so if your practice is not likely to generate malpractice claims such as bankruptcy or estate planning, you may consider a higher deductible for lower premiums.

CHAPTER 2 - SETTING UP PRACTICE

GOALS & OPPORTUNITIES CHECKLIST

Remember: Goals + Opportunities = Success

GOALS

__ *Determine Corporate Structure*

__ *Obtain Business License(s)*

__ *Apply for a Taxpayer ID Number*

__ *Assemble Support Team*

__ *Set Up Bank and Escrow Accounts*

__ *Set Up Merchant Accounts*

__ *Investigate Liability Insurance*

OPPORTUNITIES

__ *Talk to your banker (or several bankers) about your law firm. They may be an excellent resource for referrals.*

__ *Contact other attorneys in the area and ask them how they set up their corporate structure and what professional liability insurance carrier they use. The more you connect with other attorneys, they more they understand what services you offer.*

__ *Try to meet more than one accountant or CPA to talk about your practice. They may have different opinions about your corporate structure. By interviewing several, you will find one that you feel most comfortable with in advising your practice.*

"I NEVER DREAMT OF SUCCESS. I WORKED FOR IT." – ESTEE LAUDER

CHAPTER 3

SETTING UP PROCEDURES

While this may be the least fun part of creating your business, it is important to have forms and systems in place. Setting up your procedures ensures that information is current and keeps you on track for your client matters. There are many resources out there to help you. Most Bar Associations have Law Office Management Divisions with sample forms for everything from a retainer letter to a termination of representation letter.

CREATE INTAKE FORM

An intake form is a critical tool for your practice. You need to capture necessary information and relevant details on every matter. You should have sufficient information to be able to get in touch several ways and to screen for potential conflicts.

At a minimum, an intake form should include your clients' legal names, contact information, and any relevant information. The simpler the form, the better. If you have forms of several pages, a client may not complete it.

Get the basic information and fill out the rest when you meet with them. Include a section on your form where the client can tell you how they heard about your firm. This is valuable to determine which marketing efforts are working for your business. If they indicate another attorney or a client referred them, it is important to personally thank that referral source.

Here are some basic items for your client intake form:

- First and Last Names. Any Aliases.
- Address, City, County, State, ZIP

- Occupation
- Telephone (Home/Work/Cell)
- Email Address
- Immediate Family Members. This may provide a future marketing opportunity.
- Ask how they would prefer to receive communications from you.
- Other contacts. If the initial contact is not your client, record who made the initial contact and the relationship to the client.
- Details or Description of Legal Issue or Incident, including any injuries or claims.
- Any Co-Parties?
- Any Adverse Parties?
- How did they hear about you? Record if they came to you from an advertisement, mail solicitation, or legal services referral company.

SET UP A DATABASE

Consistently processing each client with your firm's intake form and adding their information to your database will help you with future contact. Too many lawyers begin their practice without thinking through this step. Trying to create a database to communicate with past clients is very time consuming, especially if you have been practicing for several years.

Not only will you use this intake form to handle your client's matter but you should also put their basic information in a database. Law firm database options are available through many vendors, so take the time to research this. If you expect your firm to stay small, consider starting with your Outlook or Gmail contacts' account.

Many larger database programs are compatible and will export information from these two programs into their system. Use your database to send correspondence, newsletters, holiday cards, annual reminders, tax or law changes that might affect them or something related to their matter.

For example, we would send letters to our estate planning clients to remind them to check their Last Will and Testament and other documents to see if there were any changes that they needed to address. This gives your clients a valuable service, but it also keeps your practice in the forefront of their minds and may lead to more business from them or someone they thought to refer to you.

CREATE NEW CLIENT CHECKLIST

Handling casework for a client has many steps. It is helpful to put together a checklist so important steps are not overlooked.

On the checklist, you should put all the necessary items needed for the completion of a matter. Not only does this keep you on track with a case, but it is helpful should you have employees who assist you on multiple matters. At a glance, you should be able to determine where you are on a matter to help with updating your client on their status and for billing purposes.

Items on a checklist may include:

- Intake Form Received
- Initial Client Meeting
- Conflicts Check Completed
- Retainer Letter Sent and Received
- Retainer Funds Deposited in Escrow
- Thank You Letter to Referral Source
- [All items or steps to relating to the handling of the specific matter such as drafting, filing, signing, copying, mailing to court or clients, archiving, etc.]

- Matter Completed
- Closing and Thank You Letter to Client
- Final Invoice
- Payment(s) Received
- Client Matter Filed and Archived

DEVELOP A CONFLICTS CHECK

Some jurisdictions require a system or at least a policy to prevent conflicts of interest. Fortunately, it is easier to determine conflicts in a small or solo practice than in a much larger firm. There are various software programs available to help with this but with a small practice, it is just as easy to create an Excel spreadsheet and use the search feature. Information that you may want to input into your database includes:

- **Client Name** (Entity Name, Personal Name, Legal Name, Maiden Name)
- **Any Co-Parties** (Entity Name, Personal Name, Legal Name, Maiden Name)
- **Adverse or Related Parties**
- **Adverse Counsel** (Attorneys & Firms) and/or **Witnesses and Experts**

If your practice is representing a husband and wife in the same matter, it is important to get informed consent. For example, you may want to put a statement in your initial retainer letter regarding a potential conflict. A sample statement might be:

CONFLICTS STATEMENT

While I can provide legal services to both you and your spouse it is critical that each of you note the following:

(i) Because I represent both of you, each of you is considered my client. Any matters disclosed to me by one will be disclosed to the other. Under the rules of Professional Conduct, I cannot agree with either one of you to withhold information from the other. Please note however that any matter which either one of you disclose to me is privileged from disclosure to third parties.

(ii) If there are differences of opinions regarding your plans I can suggest the pros and cons of the differing options. Under the rules of Professional Conduct, I cannot promote one of your positions over the other.

(iii) If a conflict should arise between the two of you that would make it difficult to represent you both, I may have to withdraw as your joint attorney and advise one or both of you to obtain independent counsel.

DETERMINE FEE STRUCTURE

All bars associations require that legal fees should be "reasonable." But what does that mean? Factors that should be considered include the time and labor required, the complexity of the legal matter, the skill and expertise of the attorney, and the comparable rate for the services in your jurisdiction among other considerations. Some jurisdictions have statutory fees of what can be charged for certain services. There may be caps on contingency fees for personal injury cases or a set schedule of fees for probating an estate. Do not neglect taking the time to research your state's statutes.

SHOULD YOU CHARGE A FLAT FEE OR HOURLY RATE?

Transactional work, such as preparing estate planning documents, real estate transactions, or business formations, may be structured as a flat fee charge. Many firms are making an effort to charge flat fees or at least provide a flat fee option to their clients. We suggest researching the local competition in your area to make the best determinations for your practice.

Clients see an advantage to knowing what something will cost them up front. The advantage to you is that flat rate fees are generally less subject to billing disputes, and you do not need to track your time for a matter.

In your retainer letter, always have a phrase or two about additional time charges if the work goes outside of the scope of the flat rate. However, there may be situations where you should charge based on an hourly rate such as a long drawn out case or a contract that must be changed several times.

When billing on an hourly basis, it is better to itemize the work done with a descriptive sentence or two rather than present a bill that says "2 hours work = $750." More details in your invoice will lead to fewer disputes with your clients. Make sure you truly document your hours worked so that you are compensated fairly. It may surprise you that a matter took longer than you anticipated.

Another note about fees: as attorneys, your time is your inventory and how you get paid. Although there is much talk about attorney's overbilling, it is just as easy to undercharge as well. While it may be nice to round down for your client's matter, you need to be fairly paid for your efforts. We found that a viable option for our firm was to create a standard fee sheet for basic services. This helps our clients understand what to expect when they agree to the fees, which eliminated client fee negotiations and disagreements.

DRAFT A RETAINER OR FEE AGREEMENT

It is highly recommended to set out the terms of your relationship with your client. A retainer letter or fee agreement outlines what the client should expect so there are no surprises or areas for dispute, especially regarding fee payment and retainers. You should highlight how your fees are calculated, either by an hourly rate or a flat fee. You should also request that your client maintain a minimum balance in their escrow account so you don't have to keep asking for money. Make sure it is in line with the scope of the representation.

You should also mention that the retainer will be held in the law firm's escrow account and any unearned balance will be refunded to the client.

Another important part of your retainer letter should address the responsibilities of the client. For example, the client should pay any fees when due, the client should keep you informed of any developments and they should respond promptly to your requests for information.

Make sure you receive the signed letter back with the client's retainer and keep this in the client's file.

SAMPLE RETAINER LETTER/FEE AGREEMENT

The purpose of this letter is to confirm based on our conversation that [FIRM NAME] will represent you in [DETAILS OF MATTER].

Our representation pursuant to this Agreement shall become effective upon your acceptance of employment.

Our rate for services performed by an attorney is $_____ per hour. You will be notified and billed for expenses incurred on your behalf.

We require an initial retainer fee of $_____ before we review the necessary information and documents or take any action related to this representation. All retainers will be deposited in the firm's trust account and will be applied toward the fees and costs incurred in this matter. We will bill against the retainer monthly; however, you will be billed for any fees and costs that exceed the retainer.

We may further require and request that you maintain a minimum balance in our trust account at all times. Upon completion of our representation, the firm will refund any excess to you.

If these rates change, we will notify you thirty (30) days in advance. It is understood that the hourly time charges include, but are not limited to: telephone conferences, office conferences, legal research, review of file materials and documents sent and received; meetings and negotiations; drafting of agreements, office memoranda and correspondence. We estimate, but cannot guarantee, that legal fees will be in the range of $_____ to $_____ for these matters. However, it is impossible to determine in advance the amount of time that will be needed to complete your case.

If this letter accurately reflects our understanding, we request that you sign the original and return it to our office along with the initial retainer fee. Unless and until we receive the signed copy of this letter, along with the full initial retainer, we may elect not to undertake any work on your behalf.

Your cooperation in this matter is very important; specifically, you must keep us informed of all relevant facts and circumstances and respond promptly to all papers sent to you.

We look forward to working with you on this matter. Please do not hesitate to give us a call at any time should you have any comments or questions about our representation.

Sincerely,

[YOUR NAME& FIRM NAME]

ACKNOWLEDGMENT OF DESIRE TO EMPLOY FIRM

I/We understand and agree to the terms set forth above and do hereby employ your services in accordance with the same, and authorize you to use our/my funds held in your trust account for attorneys' fees and costs incurred during your representation.

By: _____ Dated: _____

DRAFT COLLECTION LETTERS

Before you begin your practice, make sure you have a procedure in place to get paid. First, we would recommend not being in a collection situation. If possible, collect a retainer at your first client meeting. Clients are much more responsive if they have paid part of your fee. Keep your client updated on the status of their matter as well as your time spent and fee earned.

Clients are more receptive to paying when they have been kept informed about the work you have done. If practical, send monthly billings. Avoid surprising your client with a large billing statement that may cause the client to mistrust you. Again, putting your time into a clear fee agreement on the front end will cause less trouble when it comes time to be paid. Unfortunately, you may still run across clients that simply don't pay.

In this event, you should first send your invoice, then a statement, and then a collection letter. You should have a collection letter drafted on your laptop and ready to go. Keep in mind your time is your inventory. Review your outstanding invoices and stay on top of your clients.

SAMPLE COLLECTION LETTER

Dear _____,

Although we have contacted you about the outstanding balance on your account, we still have not heard from you. You have an outstanding balance of $_____.

The following invoice is overdue: (Enter Invoice Details)

If you have already sent payment in full, I ask that you call me and provide me specifics.

Otherwise, please call me to discuss what you plan to do to settle your account.

Thank you for your prompt attention to this matter.

If you do not get paid from your client, then you may need to send a more direct demand letter. Again, it is always better to get paid a retainer or paid upfront and hold the money in your escrow account rather than having to track down clients and demand collections.

A sample follow up collection letter is on the next page.

SAMPLE FOLLOW UP COLLECTION LETTER

Dear _____,

We have sent you several letters regarding the outstanding balance owed for our legal services.

Although we have contacted you about the outstanding balance on your account, we still have not received a response from you. You have an outstanding balance of $_____. A copy of the invoice is attached.

We are prepared to proceed with legal action if this debt is not paid. However, we would like to give you one last opportunity to pay the outstanding balance within 10 days of the date of this letter before proceeding with any legal action.

THANK REFERRAL SOURCES

Always thank referral sources in a timely manner. We found that our referral sources appreciated being thanked and being informed that we would be working with the new client.

You can keep it brief and you do not need to provide details of the representation. Handwritten notes have the most impact but you can keep a form letter on your computer.

SAMPLE THANK YOU FOR REFERRAL LETTER

Dear _____:

I wanted to personally thank you for your referral of [NEW CLIENT] to our firm.

After careful review of their situation, I am looking forward to helping them in their matter.

I appreciate the confidence you have placed in me by giving them my name. I will do my best to provide any referrals of yours with the best possible service.

As simple as this is, it is surprising to hear how much our referral sources have appreciated our gratitude. Communicating with a referral source in this way is well worth the cost of a stamp.

DRAFT CLOSING LETTER

Once you have concluded a matter for your client, be sure to send a closing letter that explains what you have done for them, if any balances are yet unpaid, and thank them for allowing you to represent them.

Summarizing the representation will clarify any disputes and serve as a record of your work. This is also a great opportunity to ask them to refer you to friends and family for future work.

SAMPLE THANK YOU LETTER TO CLIENT

Dear _____:

We wish to take this opportunity to thank you for allowing us to represent you with your matter.

We hope this matter has been concluded to your satisfaction. We would appreciate any feedback that would help us improve our services.

Our best customers come from our past clients. If you know of someone that may need our services, please have them contact us for a free initial consultation.

Thank you, again, for allowing us to represent you in this matter. If we can be of further assistance on this or any other matter, please do not hesitate to contact us.

It is also a good idea to mention the files or documents you may be retaining in your office and the files or documents you are providing to your client directly. Keep a record in your files, especially if your client is keeping any original documents.

GET FORMS & RESOURCES

When possible, don't reinvent the wheel. Standard forms such as retainer letters, fee agreements, or collection letters may be found at the ABA website **http://www.americanbar.org/resources_for_lawyers** or under the "Law Practice Management" tab (or similar menu item) on your State Bar Association's website. The official state bar websites are listed below to save you the time of looking for them. We have researched these sites and made notes below as a quick reference sheet. After reviewing the standard forms and letters, adapt these to your specific practice and needs as there is a lot of useful information to help your practice. Additionally, some state bar websites have leadership academies or mentoring programs that are geared to those opening a new firm.

Note: if your state does not have a particularly good website for law practice management or none at all, check out other states' sites. Chances are they will have something helpful for you. Keep in mind, the term "Lawyer's Assistance" generally means lawyers dealing with substance abuse or mental health issues.

STATE BY STATE GUIDE TO FORMS & RESOURCES

ALABAMA
www.alabar.org/programs-departments/leadership-forum
Note: At this writing, they do not have a practice management site but rather a leadership forum.

ALASKA
www.alaskabar.org/servlet/content/New_Lawyers_1 49.html
Note: At this writing, they do not have a practice management site but a forum section for new lawyers.

ARIZONA
www.azbar.org/professionaldevelopment/practice20 /
Note: At this writing, they have a free and confidential 30 minute tutorial for practice management.

CALIFORNIA
www.calbar.ca.gov/Attorneys/Sections/Law-Practice-Management-Technology
Note: At this writing, there is a section for Practice Management and Technology. They also have guides on law practice management in California for purchase.

COLORADO
www.cobar.org/lpm
Note: At this writing, they have topics on law practice management.

CONNECTICUT
www.ctbar.org/page/LPMResource
Note: At this writing, they have a Law Practice Management Resource Center.

DELAWARE

www.dsba.org/pages/sections-of-the-bar

Note: At this writing, there is a Small Firms & Solo Practitioners Section.

DISTRICT OF COLUMBIA

www.dcbar.org/bar-resources/practice-management-advisory-service

Note: At this writing, the Practice Management Advisory Service puts on a Practice Management Seminar.

FLORIDA

www.pri.floridabar.org

Note: At this writing, they have a Practice Resource Institute.

GEORGIA

www.gabar.org/committeesprogramssections/programs/lpm/index.cfm

Note: At this writing, they have a Solo & Small Firm Institute.

HAWAII

http://hsba.org/HSBA/For_Lawyers/Leadership%20Institute.aspx

Note: At this writing, they do not have a practice management website but they do have a leadership institute.

IDAHO

www.isb.idaho.gov/member_services/memberservices.html

Note: At this writing, they have resources on their member services page.

ILLINOIS

www.isba.org/soloinstitute

Note: At this writing, they have a Solo & Small Firm Practice Institute.

INDIANA
www.indybar.org/index.cfm?pg=SoloSmallFirm-HomePage
Note: At this writing, they have a Solo & Small Firm home page with resources.

IOWA
www.iowabar.org/?page=PracticeTools
Note: At this writing, they have a page with practice resources and tools.

KANSAS
www.ksbar.org/?lomap
Note: At this writing, they have a Law Practice Management Assistance Program.

KENTUCKY
www.kbagps.org
Note: At this writing, they do not have a practice management site but they do provide mentors.

LOUISIANA
www.lsba.org/Members/PracticeManagement.aspx
Note: At this writing, they have a Practice Management program and a Practice Aid Guide.

MAINE
www.mainebar.org
Note: At this writing, they do not have a practice management site but they do have a Leadership Academy.

MARYLAND
www.msba.org/practicemanagement/default.aspx
Note: On their practice management site, they provide articles and webinars.

MASSACHUSETTS
www.massbar.org/member-groups/sections/law-practice-management/
Note: At this writing, they practice management site and a Leadership Academy.

MICHIGAN
www.michbar.org/pmrc/content

Note: At this writing, they have a Practice Management Helpline and produce a Law Practice Today e-zine.

MINNESOTA
www.mnbar.org/tools-online-resources

Note: At this writing, they have online tools and resources.

MISSISSIPPI
www.msbar.org/programs-affiliates/law-practice-management-resource-center.aspx

Note: At this writing, they do not have a practice management site but they do have a Leadership Academy.

MISSOURI
www.mobar.org/lpmonline

Note. At this writing, they have an online Law Practice Management resource.

MONTANA
www.montanabar.org

Note: At this writing, they do not have a practice management site.

NEBRASKA
http://www.nebar.com/?ProgramsServices

Note: At this writing, they have some practice tools and manuals and a Leadership Academy.

NEVADA
www.nvbar.org/member-services-3895/sections/solo-and-small-practice-section

Note: At this writing, they have a Solo and Small Practice Section.

NEW HAMPSHIRE
www.nhbar.org/for-members/login.asp

Note: As this writing, you will need to be a member of the New Hampshire Bar Association to log onto this site.

NEW JERSEY
www.njsba.com
Note: At this writing, they have a Solo and Small Firm Section and a Law Office Management Committee.

NEW MEXICO
www.nmbar.org/nmstatebar/Membership/Law_Practice_Management/Nmstatebar/About_Us/Law_Practice_Management/Law_Practice_Management.aspx
Note: at this writing, they have Law Practice Management Resources.

NEW YORK
www.nysba.org/LawPracticeManagement
Note: At this writing, they have a Law Practice Management website.

NORTH CAROLINA
www.ncbar.org/members/practice-management
Note: At this writing, they have a Center for Practice Management with links and webinars.

NORTH DAKOTA
www.sband.org
Note: They have a Mentorship Program and a Protect Your Practice Toolkit to help establish and protect your online image.

OHIO
www.ohiobar.org/ForLawyers/MemberResources/PracticeResources/Pages/PracticeResources.aspx
Note: At this writing, they have a Practice Resources Page and an Office Keeper Guide for your firm.

OKLAHOMA
www.okbar.org/members/MAP.aspx
Note: At this writing, they have a Management Assistance Program.

OREGON
www.osbar.org/forms

Note: At this writing, they do not have a practice management site but they do have a forms library.

PENNSYLVANIA
http://www.pabar.org/public/lpm/lpm.asp#Contents

Note: At this writing, they have a Law Practice Management Area and Solo and Small Firm Practice Section.

RHODE ISLAND
www.ribar.com/Login/Login.aspx?ReturnUrl=/Members%20Only%20Area/Online%20Attorney%20Resources%20(OAR).aspx

Note: At this writing, there is an online resource site accessible for bar association members only.

SOUTH CAROLINA
http://www.scbar.org/Bar-Members/Practice-Management-PMAP

Note: At this writing, they have a Practice Management Assistance Program with resources and a telephone and email hotline.

SOUTH DAKOTA
www.sdbar.org

Note: At this writing, they do not have a practice management site.

TENNESSEE
http://www.tba.org/node/66492

Note: At this writing, they have a "Solo Practice Toolkit."

TEXAS
www.texaslawpracticemanagement.com

Note: At this writing, they have a Law Practice Management website.

UTAH
www.utahbar.org
Note: At this writing, they do not have a practice management site but provide links to resources.

VERMONT
www.vtbar.org
Note: At this writing, they do not have a practice management site but have a Solo and Small Firm Conference.

VIRGINIA
www.vba.org/?page=practice_management
Note: At this writing, they have a Law Practice Management Division.

WASHINGTON
www.wsba.org/Resources-and-Services/LOMAP
Note: At this writing they have a Law Office Management Assistance Program.

WEST VIRGINIA
www.wvbar.org
Note: At this writing, they do not have a practice management site but have a Solo Practitioner and Small Firm Committee.

WISCONSIN
http://www.wisbar.org/Pages/default.aspx
Note: At this writing, they have a "Practice411" tab for which you must be a member of the Wisconsin bar to access.

WYOMING
www.wyomingbar.org/law-office-self-audit-checklist
Note: At this writing, they do not have a practice management site but they do have a practice management "self-audit" checklist.

ABA RESOURCES

Solo and Small Firm Resource Center
www.americanbar.org/portals/solo_home/practice-management2.html

Forms Library
www.americanbar.org/groups/gpsolo/resources/solo_small_firm_formslibrary.html

CHAPTER 3 - SETTING UP PROCEDURES

GOALS & OPPORTUNITIES CHECKLIST

Remember: Goals + Opportunities = Success

GOALS

__ *Develop Intake Form*

__ *Set Up Database*

__ *Create New Client Checklist*

__ *Develop Conflicts Check*

__ *Determine Fee Structure*

__ *Draft Retainer Letter or Fee Agreement*

__ *Draft Collection Letters*

__ *Thank Referral Sources*

__ *Draft Closing Letter*

__ *Create Forms*

OPPORTUNITIES

__ *Before you develop a fee structure investigate what your competition is doing. Are your rates in line with the market or too high or too low? Reach out to other attorneys and ask them.*

__ *Contact your state bar association and find their resources for practice management. Take advantage of mentoring programs or education for law practice management.*

"THERE IS NO ELEVATOR TO SUCCESS. YOU HAVE TO TAKE THE STAIRS." - ANONYMOUS

CHAPTER 4

SETTING UP SYSTEMS

The good news for solo practitioners is that there are so many practice management options available to help save you time and money. Activate those law school research skills and determine what options are available to assist with building and growing your law firm. The best part is that these systems can be managed from your laptop or mobile phone thereby supporting your "mobile law office."

FIND ACCOUNTING SOFTWARE

When evaluating which accounting system or software to use, check with your CPA or accountant. They are intimately familiar with what might work well for your business. Generally, the software is easy to set up and use.

Unless your accountant or CPA suggests otherwise, we have used and recommend QuickBooks Pro by Intuit. It is easy to use and most accountants and bookkeepers are familiar with it. It also allows you to generate professional looking invoices, statements, and collection letters from the program as well as handle accounts payable and payroll. It can also be integrated into some practice management software.

COMPARE MANAGEMENT PROGRAMS

Practice and case management software programs help you handle all aspects of your law firm including billing, conflict checking, time tracking, case managing, task managing, client communication, calendaring, and document assembly. Most utilize the cloud and have mobile apps for your phones so you can manage your firm from anywhere.

Investigate the upfront fees and monthly fees for the services you're interested in utilizing. Some have large startup fees but low monthly fees, while others do not require a startup cost but the monthly fee may be higher.

Request a demonstration or take advantage of a free trial to see what works best for your practice.

PRACTICE MANAGEMENT SOFTWARE

AbacusLaw   www.abacusnext.com

AmicusAttorney   www.amicusattorney.com

ActionStep   www.actionstep.com

CosmoLex   www.cosmolex.com

Clio   www.goclio.com

FirmCentral   www.firmcentral.com

FirmManager   www.firmmanager.com

HoudiniEsq.   www.houdiniesq.com

Leap   www.leap.us

MyCase   www.mycase.com

ProLaw   www.prolaw.com

SET UP A VOICE MAIL ACCOUNT

Who needs a receptionist? This is one expense you can do without. Messages don't get lost or miscommunicated if they are going directly to you. If anything, our clients loved the fact they could reach us directly or go to our voice mail.

If you don't have a dedicated cell phone for your law firm, there are many options for a virtual business line that can be directed to your email, phone or smartphone. Most Voice Over Internet Providers (VOIPs) can provide custom greetings, multiple voicemail boxes, toll-free numbers, & call logs.

VOICE MAIL PROVIDERS

8x8	www.8x8.com
Grasshopper	www.grasshopper.com
OOMA Office	www.ooma.com
RingCentral	www.ringcentral.com
Vonage	www.vonagebusiness.com

FIND LEGAL RESEARCH RESOURCES

Legal research has become much easier with online resources. Some providers charge a monthly fee, but they offer a free trial to test run their services first. Check with your State Bar Association to see if you have free or discounted access to certain providers as part of your benefits of being a member.

LEGAL RESEARCH RESOURCES

FastCase	www.fastcase.com
FindLaw	www.findlaw.com
Justia	www.justia.com
LexisNexis	www.lexisnexis.com
Westlaw	www.westlaw.com

SET UP DOCUMENT PREPARATION

You should automate the creation of standard legal documents that you would use frequently, such as contracts, leases, wills, and letters. You may find free templates by searching the Internet or your State Bar Association's website. Most of the Practice Management Software Programs mentioned above feature document assembly for your practice area.

You can pay per document from such legal document preparation sites as Nolo (**www.nolo.com**) or Rocket Lawyer **(www.rocketlawyer.com)** or use more sophisticated and detailed programs to make your operation more efficient.

DOCUMENT PREPARATION SOFTWARE

HotDocs			www.hotdocs.com

MyCase			www.mycase.com

ProDoc			www.prodoc.com

Thomson Reuters
www.legalsolutions.thomsonreuters.com/law-products

RETAIN & BACKUP FILES

Your primary concern, other than losing your hard work and important client files, is confidentiality. Make sure whatever filing and backup system you use, it is safe from hackers. Check with your State Bar Association to see if there are any rules regarding the backup of files, especially if it is cloud-based storage. You should also have a fireproof cabinet for client files that can be locked and held in a secure location.

CLOUD-BASED STORAGE SITES

Box.com	www.box.com
Carbonite	www.carbonite.com
DropBox	www.dropbox.com
Idrive	www.idrive.com
OneDrive	www.OneDrive.com
Mozy	www.Mozy.com

CHAPTER 4 - SYSTEMS & SOFTWARE

GOALS & OPPORTUNITIES CHECKLIST

Remember: Goals + Opportunities = Success

GOALS

___ *Find Accounting Software*

___ *Compare Management Programs*

___ *Set Up a Voice Mail Account*

___ *Find Research Resources*

___ *Set Up Document Preparation*

___ *Retain and Back Up Files*

OPPORTUNITIES

___ *Talk to other attorneys and ask them what software and systems they use. This is not necessarily proprietary information and many attorneys will be happy to share what has worked for them and compare notes with you.*

> "NEVER, NEVER, NEVER GIVE UP." – WINSTON CHURCHILL.

CHAPTER 5

MARKETING & GETTING CLIENTS

The most difficult thing an attorney should do, and is never taught in law school, is to "sell yourself." You may be the most brilliant legal mind in your area, but if you don't promote yourself, potential clients may never know. Talk to EVERYBODY about the law you practice. You never know where you may get your next client. You may have to get out of your comfort zone but realize that you have value to offer and people should know about your services.

KNOW YOUR BAR RULES

Advertising and marketing is important for any business, but it can prove tricky for attorneys. You must familiarize yourself with your State Bar Association's rules of advertising and solicitation.

Generally, the bar rules will refer to all forms of communication seeking legal employment such as newspapers, brochures, press releases, television, radio, direct mail, electronic mail and Internet communications like websites, banner ads, social networking, blogs, etc. Even announcements or invitations about your sponsored seminars are subject to the rules. Many communications such as print or television ads, must be submitted to your state bar for approval. So called, "Tombstone Ads" are an exception. This is where you would only include your most basic information, for example:

- Name of Law Firm
- Name of Lawyer
- Office locations and hours of operation
- Licenses Held
- Date of Admission to the State Bar
- If you speak a foreign language or accept credit cards
- If you provide a free consultation

Again, for any advertising or marketing communications, make sure it falls in line with the rules of advertising and solicitation.

A note about solicitation: Since you went to law school you probably know you cannot "ambulance chase" clients. Handing out business cards in hospitals or accident scenes is strictly prohibited. Similarly, you can't put your business card under windshields. Additionally, there are also strict guidelines on sending out unsolicited direct mail to prospective clients. Make sure you know your rules!

A note about referrals: Your best source of clients will be from past clients. Hopefully you will get many referrals from satisfied clients. You may also get referrals from others who know you and know you'll do a good job for a potential client. As grateful as you may be for these referrals, you are prohibited from paying non-lawyers a referral fee. However, under the ABA Model Rules of Professional Conduct, adopted by most states, an attorney may share fees with another "competent" attorney if the fees are in proportion to the services performed by each lawyer and the client agrees to the arrangement.

A note about Lawyer Referral services: You may list your practice with a Lawyer Referral Service which markets to the public and provides a list of attorneys from which to consider. You must make sure that the Lawyer Referral Service complies with your State Bar Association's rules of advertising and solicitation. Also, be aware that most Lawyer Referral Services require that you have professional liability insurance.

A note about Pre-Paid Legal services: You can be a resource for a pre-paid legal plan. Pre-paid legal plans are usually offered as an employee benefit. You agree to a set fee schedule for certain legal services, such as a drafting of a will or representation for a traffic violation. The company will refer clients to you and pay you directly. This will give you experience and possibly those clients will retain you for other services not covered in the plan. Hopefully they will refer others to you. The downside is that you will be paid a fraction of your market rate, and you may need a certain level of professional liability insurance to be a part of a pre-paid referral plan. However, it may be something to consider if you are just starting your practice.

CRAFT YOUR "ELEVATOR SPEECH"

The most important rule of marketing is effectively communicating what you do. Do you have an "Elevator Speech?" That is, can you quickly introduce yourself and describe your services in a quick, succinct, attention-grabbing, understandable manner? Just telling people your name and proclaiming, "I'm a lawyer" does not help you sell yourself.

First, identify and communicate what problems you solve. For example, we found by that by introducing ourselves as "Estate Planning Attorneys," we did not connect with most people because (1) they did not know what estate planning attorneys did or (2) assumed that they needed a certain net worth (the word "estate" conjures up manor houses) to require the services of such an attorney. Instead, we now explain that we help families and small businesses prepare for significant life events like disability and death and give them peace of mind. By phrasing it that way, it would likely begin a conversation where someone might talk about a situation that was happening in his or her own family or business.

Tailor your speech to manage the perceptions of your field. For example, instead of introducing yourself as a "divorce attorney," which may conjure negative stereotypes or preconceived ideas, you say, "I keep the peace! I help families navigate the tough issues surrounding divorce to make everyone happy."

Engage the listener. Explain what you do, but try to evoke a response. For example, if you are the divorce attorney, you could say "Do you know anyone who needs a peacekeeper?"

The more creative your introduction, the better it will be remembered and passed on to others. There are many resources on the Internet on how to effectively craft your "elevator speech" and put your best foot forward.

CREATE A STANDOUT BUSINESS CARD

You know the typical lawyer's business card: all black and white type, all block letters, usually just the Attorney's name, address, phone and email. Not much imagination or excitement there.

Make your business card work for you. You want your business card to be a dynamic advertisement. Just like the "Elevator Speech," you want people to understand what you do and know exactly how you can help them. Of course, you need to have your basic information of name, address, telephone number, but you should also include your website address, your business' Facebook page address, your blog address, Twitter, etc.

Put a catchy tag line under your firm's name. For example, if you are an attorney who primarily works with small businesses, you can put "I'm your in-house counsel." Of course, check with your State Bar Association rules of what can and cannot be on your business card.

Keep in mind the brand you want to create and your target audience when crafting your business card. You can be colorful while still being professional.

Don't forget to use the back of your card! It is not that much more expensive to have printing on the back and it is the perfect spot to either list the areas of practice that you handle and/or have a "Call to Action." You know the standard TV call to action: "DON'T DELAY! ACT NOW!" Of course, you may want a more subtle message to prompt people to reach out to you. For example, you could put, "Call today for a free one-hour consultation" or "Call me for my free article: *10 Things You Should Know If You've Been Involved in a Car Accident.*"

DESIGN A PROFESSIONAL WEBSITE

The Yellow Pages are a thing of the past. Today, you are not considered a legitimate enterprise unless you have a website. Make it great!

Everyone Googles everything now, so it is most likely you will be screened by potential clients on the web. They will look at your website <u>even if</u> they have been referred by someone else.

Check out other attorney websites, especially those of solo practitioners and lawyers in your field. You will find terrific ones and terrible ones. Don't be too fancy with graphics or videos that take too long to load. You want your website to be clear and friendly (remember some people are put off by lawyers). Have a photo of yourself and detail your background and experience. This will be a primary way for a client to determine if they will hire you.

Make sure you have good content and advice – give potential clients value for visiting your page. Feature articles on your expertise or display your blog with relevant information (more about blogging later). Consider the latest trend of creating short videos to answer frequently asked questions or to present yourself to potential clients. A quick introduction video on your website can showcase your personality making you more approachable.

Highlight your visibility in the community. For example, if you have written articles, include links to them on your webpage. If you will be speaking at an event, put that event information on your webpage. This is not so much to have people read your articles or have people come to your speaking engagements. It is instead meant to communicate that you are an attorney who is sought out for advice. Use your website for your legitimacy or "street credibility."

Do you offer a free consultation? Tell your viewers. Do you offer flat rate legal services? Show your packages. As a consumer yourself, isn't price a factor when you choose someone from a website? People like to know what to expect.

If you don't have the time or computer expertise, you can hire a professional website developer. However, there are many companies that make it easy to create your own website. We were shocked how simple it was to design our own website and we enjoyed the flexibility of changing and updating it to suit our needs.

For example, as part of our marketing efforts, we did a great deal of public speaking. Since we could change our website whenever we wanted, we would post dates of our monthly speaking engagements and seminars. Often these changes could be done in a matter of minutes. This was much easier than having to call a contracted webmaster whenever we needed to make such updates.

WEBSITE CREATOR SITES

Go Daddy	www.godaddy.com
SquareSpace	www.squarespace.com
WEBS	www.webs.com
Website Builder	www.websitebuilder.com
Wix	www.wix.com
WordPress	www.wordpress.com

ADVERTISE YOUR WEBSITE

Once you have your website up and running, you will want to drive traffic to your site. Learn about search engine optimization (SEO), and either familiarize yourself with how to integrate SEO into your website or hire someone to help increase your website's visibility.

You can do a lot on your own to promote your website. Put your website address on all your literature, letters, business cards, and advertisements.

Add your website address to every email you send out, both business and personal. We are constantly communicating with people inside our community about social events, children's activities, and volunteering opportunities, and often the subject of our business does not come up in our conversations. If you email these groups for any reason, include your website address below your signature line. Don't neglect opportunities to gently get your website address out to people.

LEGAL SEARCH SITES

Avvo	www.avvo.com
FindLaw	www.findlaw.com
LawGuru	www.lawguru.com
Law.net	www.law.net
Law Firm Directory	www.lawfirmdirectory.org
Lawyers	www.lawyers.com
Martindale	www.martindale.com
Nolo	www.nolo.com
SuperLawyers	www.superlawyers.com

Check with your local chamber of commerce or town business directory to see if they will list your business information.

BUSINESS DIRECTORY SITES

GoogleMyBusiness	www.google.com/business
Manta	www.manta.com
Yelp	www.yelp.com

Some of them may charge a fee to list; others will give you a free listing.

INCLUDE A DISCLAIMER! While you want to give some tips and general information about your services, make sure on the home page of your website you include a disclaimer to help avoid liability.

SAMPLE DISCLAIMER

This site is for informational purposes only and does not constitute legal advice. Please consult an attorney for advice about your individual situation. Feel free to contact us by electronic mail, letters, or phone calls. Contacting us does not create an attorney-client relationship. Until an attorney-client relationship is established, do not send any confidential information to us.

BLOG ON YOUR AREA OF EXPERTISE

Should you blog? Many attorneys have blogs as part of their website. It is a way to introduce your expertise and personality to people who have never met you. It may also drive traffic to your website that results in new clients. However, it is not mandatory to blog to have a successful practice.

We would suggest that solo practitioners should only blog if they (1) love to write (2) have something of value to write about and (3) can truly make the time commitment to keep blogs fresh.

What should you blog about? Tips about your practice area and interesting developments in the laws or headlines that are relevant to your practice. If you are an estate planner, you could blog about changes to estate taxes or recent stories of celebrity deaths and if they had good estate plans. If you are a family law attorney, you could blog about how to handle children and custody issues during a divorce.

Here are some things to keep in mind when blogging:

- **CONTENT IS KING.** Although conventional wisdom says blog posts should be relatively short, 300-700 words, you don't have to get caught up on actual word count. If you need to present a topic in 2,000 words, then it is best to do so. Studies show that longer posts that are heavily researched and present data or statistics are shared or tweeted more than brief posts. Sometimes, a motivational bit of information is just as effective. Blogging effectiveness is constantly changing so be certain to keep your marketing current.

- **FOCUS ON 1 TOPIC OR MAIN IDEA.** People generally scan blog posts. Some studies have shown that people generally read only 20% of a blog. Use headings and images to be visually interesting and to break up text, and include emphasis points that are easy to see during a skim. Infographics are becoming more popular as they are easy to read and understand.

- **END POSTS WITH A QUESTION OR CALL TO ACTION.** For example, if you are a business attorney you could end all your posts with a tag line: "Contact me for my article '10 Things to Do When Starting a Business.'" If your article was about common mistakes made when setting up a business, you could ask, "What do you wish you knew before setting up your business?" Include your contact information at the end of each blog.

- **CREATE A BLOG RESERVE.** You may have great intentions to keep to a certain posting schedule, but then you become busy and fall behind. Other times you may be on a creative roll and have several ideas for blog posts. You should write a few blog posts to keep in reserve in case you become busy with clients. You can use the blog interface to schedule when blog posts are published and that makes it simple to plan a few months in advance. Remain mindful of the calendar, as you may not want to schedule posts during holidays when your clients may not be free to look at them. Alternatively, use the calendar to your advantage. If you are a tax or business attorney you can schedule tax tips around tax season.

Check your State Bar Association's Rules of Professional Conduct regarding blogs. Most jurisdictions consider blogs to be advertising and therefore must follow the rules of lawyer advertising and solicitation.

With a click of a key, you can link your blog post to your Facebook, Twitter, LinkedIn, or Instagram accounts.

BLOG SITES

Blogger   www.blogger.com

Wix   www.wix.com

WordPress   www.wordpress.com

EMBRACE SOCIAL MEDIA

Insert eye roll here. Back when many of us started the practice of law, social media was an unheard-of concept. Now it is a large force in the marketplace, like it or not, it is here to stay.

Social media levels the playing field for client acquisition. The better presence you have on the web, the better you can compete with the larger name firms. Additionally, social media sites are free to join so you can stretch your marketing dollars and keep your expenses low which is critical for a new practice.

Having connections through Facebook, Twitter, Instagram, LinkedIn, etc., gives your firm credibility. It shows you are current with modern ways to communicate and you can display your knowledge with content. People hire attorneys based on their comfort level. You may have heard the saying: "People hire lawyers, not law firms." Social media allows you to showcase your personality which is helpful information for clients deciding whether to hire you.

Before diving into social media outlets, develop a plan:
- What do you want to achieve?
- Who is your target market?
- What social media do they use?
- How can social media reach them?
- How can I tell what works?

You should consider how you want to present your business on the many social media outlets. If you choose one or more options, set a realistic schedule of how many posts, tweets, or articles you will create.

Set aside one day each week to spend no more than 20-30 minutes on creating social media content. The number of posts is much less important than the content. What should be done daily is checking for comments and responding to any comments or messages. Even if someone posts a brief comment or likes your post, reply to their comment and thank them for reading. The key to social media is engagement. If someone responds to you, make sure to promptly respond back.

It is also important to look at what impact your posts are making. This is done by studying analytics which tell you how many people viewed your article or post, liked it, or shared it. Many social media sites display analytics for you to review. If you notice that there is a certain topic that gets more interest or a social media platform that creates more engagement, focus your efforts on expanding those. Conversely, if there is no engagement on a social media site, maybe your target audience does not use that site. If you can determine where your target audience spends most of their time on social media, you have struck gold.

Spend some time looking at how others have successfully used social media to promote their services and develop their following. See how you can adopt some of those strategies into your own social marketing plan.

FACEBOOK

Facebook is an easy way to get started in social media. You can set up a Facebook page dedicated to your firm that lists all your contact information. You can include a headshot of yourself and a short biography of you and/or your firm. Within the information you provide, it is important to include a brief disclaimer that any articles or posts are not intended as legal advice, every case is different, and any reviews do not guarantee outcomes.

With a Facebook business page, you can provide links to interesting articles, give updates on laws or your practice, and set up invitations to your speaking engagements or events.

If you blog, you can link your blogs to Facebook so that as blog posts are published, they will also show up on your page feed. This is another way for a potential client to see your personality and expertise.

You can put a Facebook icon on your website to encourage clients to like your page. On your Facebook business page, there is a section where clients can leave reviews.

We never considered having a presence on Facebook until our clients began asking us if we were on Facebook. If there was an article or tip they found could benefit someone else, it was an easy way for the client to forward the information to others.

Once your business page is set up, you can send invitations for people you know to like your page or follow you. For professional reasons, it is better not to mix your personal page with your business page. Your clients don't need to know what you ate for dinner and they likely don't want to see photos of your cat. It is also a good idea to keep clients as friends on your business page and not your personal page.

LINKEDIN

LinkedIn is another popular way to get information about yourself and your practice out in cyberspace. It is also platform that clients can easily comment on and recommend your skills. You can post any speaking engagements or publications that boost your image as an industry guru. You can also post articles or items that you think would be of interest to your audience and draw attention to your practice.

LinkedIn is also a good way to connect to referral sources. Think about everyone you know from alumni groups, to clubs, to fraternal organizations. It is an easy way to promote yourself and highlight what you do.

Use LinkedIn to get in front of your target market. Once you have identified who your potential client is, join groups that you think they would join and see what is of interest to them.

TWITTER

The advantage of Twitter is that the posts or "tweets" are limited in character length. Your tweets can convey a quick message or link back to an article on your blog or webpage. You can follow others in your practice area to learn of new developments. Others can follow you so you can build up an audience for your brand.

In fact, you should not use Twitter to promote your firm but to promote you as an individual. Show your interest and knowledge about certain topics. Start conversations about the areas you handle. Respond to the tweets you receive to continue engagement.

Another advantage of Twitter is that you don't always have to come up with original content. You can re-tweet articles that you find are well written and beneficial to your audience.

Use Twitter for research purposes as well. Find out who the successful lawyers follow. Learn from others and mimic the strategies they use to advertise their brand.

INSTAGRAM

Instagram is a social platform that allows you to share photos and short videos (one minute in length). A case could be made for Instagram if (1) you use it and love it, or (2) your target market is primarily younger adults. Set up an Instagram account for your business with a profile that links you to your website. With Instagram, you can reflect more of your personality and sense of humor.

What should you post on Instagram? Since Instagram is a visual medium, you must be creative. You can share photos of yourself in a conference room or a coffee shop waiting for a client, or show yourself in different parts of town to illustrate that you are truly mobile.

You can share inspirational quotes or funny quips. You can share a quick tip or legal fact. You can even post ridiculous laws that are still on the books, the point of Instagram is to pique someone's interest so they find out who you are.

Instagram is not the place for selling. For example, a DUI defense attorney may have better results by posting a photo of a breathalyzer device with the caption "What should you do before this?" A viewer will be intrigued and click on the photo to be linked to your information. That is engagement. Posting a card with your name, phone number and the caption "DUI Lawyer" is not engagement.

A note about hashtags: Hashtags or posting a pound sign (#) with a keyword is a powerful way for social media networks to organize data and for you to reach your audience. When you are posting an article, you can add hashtags with keywords that relate to your topic or would target your audience. For example, if you are a family law attorney in Denver and write an article about "5 Things to Do Before a Divorce" you might post the article with hashtag #divorce, #familylaw, #denver.

YOUTUBE

Many lawyers use YouTube as an inexpensive way to create short infomercials for their practice. If you enjoy that medium, you can post short videos about your practice or give general legal information. If you are going to use YouTube, look at what other attorneys have posted as examples of what to do and not do. Only proceed if you can put together a professional video that shows you in the best light.

Consider a short introduction video that you can imbed on your practice's website. A 1-2 minute video, can establish a "know, like and trust" factor. You become more authentic and human to your audience and you can make a real connection. A video showcases your personality which is important in hiring a lawyer.

Nicole Abboud, of Abboud Media, helps lawyers build their brand and grow their practice through video marketing. She advises when doing a short video to start with the "story of you." Don't recite your resume and qualifications. Engage your viewer with an interesting story about why you do what you do and how you can help them. Or grab their attention with an interesting statistic or something that they did not know. Then introduce yourself and your background. Know the purpose of your video: are you educating, informing or entertaining? Finally, give a call to action. Do you want them to call you for legal services? Subscribe to your newsletter?

Although these are highly popular social media platforms, consider the professional image you want to convey and what likelihood your time into these will result in potential clients.

SEEK OUT LIVE PRESENTATIONS

While this idea may seem terrifying, sharing your expertise and knowledge with others is a great way to market your services.

Check out local Speakers Groups, Rotary Clubs, and Chamber of Commerce Groups to see if they need speakers with your expertise. For the purposes of marketing to families with young children, we found it was effective to speak to Mom's clubs and church groups. Through these groups, we met our "target" audience and we received very positive responses from our presentations.

Keep in mind not to "sell" at speaking engagements. That only puts people off. Instead of selling, deliver tips and solid content so that the audience perceives value for the time and attention they are giving you. At our presentations, we basically tried to explain what documents such as a Will, Power of Attorney, Health Care Surrogate, and Living Will do and do not do. We would discuss tips for choosing the right guardian for their children. We avoided using scare tactics or horror stories to get calls to action. People appreciated that we gave our time to explain difficult concepts about estate planning. Most of our talks aimed at taking the mystery out of estate planning and clearing up misconceptions. We would lay out information that would led to in-depth questions, which often led to new clients.

We even created our own live presentations called "Coffee Talk." Since we wanted to reach small business owners in our area, we wanted to create a forum to network with them. We presented legal topics of interest to small businesses and invited business owners to attend. They would buy a cup of coffee and we would give a brief seminar and then answer questions. They would invite their business friends and the group got larger. The business owners would even network with each other. The coffee shop was happy to let us use the space free of charge because it increased business for them.

DEVELOP STRATEGIC PARTNERS

As attorneys, we encounter many professionals such as accountants, CPAs, financial planners, insurance agents, bank executives, business owners, etc. You should find professionals in your community that have the same values and dedication to clients that you do.

Cultivate relationships with those professionals. Meet them for lunch or a coffee, and ask them what his or her "perfect" client looks like. Keep that in mind if someone you know could benefit from his or her services. At the same time, communicate your target market. Many clients appreciate a referral to an investment advisor or accountant that you would trust. In turn, your "sources" will provide you with potential clients as well.

It is a good idea to find as many sources as possible for the best possible match. For example, a bookkeeper or small accounting firm may better serve a small business rather than a large CPA firm. Similarly, there are many types of financial advisors, those that charge a fee for consulting and others that have free advisory services but make commissions from account balances or transactions.

JOIN NETWORKING GROUPS

Networking is critical to your success. People must know you and truly understand what you offer if they are to refer business to you. People should know your "elevator speech."

There are traditional networking groups like local chambers of commerce, rotary clubs, and local business-to-business groups as well as new groups through "Meet Ups" or online meeting groups.

Think outside the box. Be active in your community by coaching sports, participating in beach or park clean ups, and linking up with other entrepreneurs. Find the local chapter of your alumni clubs.

Choose where you want to invest your time. Continuing to attend the same group meetings promotes deeper relationships rather than spreading yourself too thin over many groups. Consider putting together your own networking group of professionals you would like to get referrals from.

CREATE A NETWORKING GROUP

As entrepreneurs, we encountered those business-to-business groups in which only one industry could be represented, dues had to be paid, meetings were mandatory and you had to make at least one referral or one introduction a month. What a hassle!

Instead, we decided to find our own group of professional women who did not have the time or inclination for that commitment and did not want to be forced to make referrals in order to remain in a group.

By starting our own network of like-minded professionals, we supported each other and provided business wisdom, business start-up support and client leads.

We met once a week for one hour to present our challenges of the week and workshop solutions amongst each other. Although we were attorneys, our group included a coffee shop owner, a real estate broker, a PR and marketing professional, and a chiropractor. Although we were in remarkably different businesses, we all had common issues of employee matters, collection issues, dealing with difficult clients, etc. We called ourselves: *"The Ladies of the Round Table."* It was an invaluable resource where we would trade ideas of what has worked or hasn't worked for us. We would also set individual weekly goals and reported our success (or failure) to make sure we kept on task.

Prior to each meeting we would have to complete a brief questionnaire:

- Name an accomplishment, goal achieved, important contact made or problem fixed this week.

- Name one or more things you believe held you back from being more productive this week, and why?

- What is your number one goal to achieve next week?

- Share one "nugget" of knowledge you acquired this week or how you solved a problem.

- Please share one need or request (personal or business) with the group (contact within a certain company, name for a caregiver, recommendation for a service, etc.)

- What do you want to learn this week?

We would review each member's answers before the meeting and during the meeting we offered advice and support. This exercise would hold our members and ourselves accountable. If we mentioned our goal was to follow up on collections or update our website, we would be motivated to complete it before the next meeting. Having others review our goals and progress was daunting at times, but it challenged us to meet our goals.

This was a unique, critical factor in growing our law practice.

Another idea for networking is to host an open house. Attorney friends of ours would host a quarterly coffee and bagel event an invited all the attorneys they knew. It turned out to be very well attended and attorneys had the chance to meet other attorneys they might not ordinarily meet. If you have a mobile practice, you can host an event at a coffee shop or team up with an attorney you know and offer to co-host an event.

WRITE ARTICLES

Write articles on your specialty and see about free placement in newspapers, magazines, blogs, or websites. Everyone is looking for content. As with live presentations, make sure you are not "selling," but rather offer valuable advice and practical tips. Keep your audience in mind and write topics that would be of interest to them.

Keep it simple with bullet points or short paragraphs. You should write clearly and define words as your audience may not have your legal knowledge.

At the end of the article you can put a description of your practice and your contact information as part of your byline. There are many tips you could provide the public on your area of expertise. Even general articles give you exposure to potential clients.

WRITE A NEWSLETTER

The best referral source is your former clients. Keep in touch with them by sending a monthly, quarterly or even annual newsletter with legal updates, helpful articles or tips. You will be perceived as giving them value and they will keep your name and services in their mind. They may also pass along your newsletter to others. There are simple newsletter templates in Microsoft Word that you could mail or email to your clients.

A helpful resource for newsletters is a website called Constant Contact (**www.constantcontact.com**), which for a small monthly fee, offers newsletter templates and programs to send out communications by email. The program gives you information on how many people open your emails and click on your links. There is also an opt-out feature that lets you know who would prefer not to be contacted.

Also, the website Mail Chimp (**www.mailchimp.com**) offers a free email service for a limited number of subscribers.

CHAPTER 5 – MARKETING & GETTING CLIENTS

GOALS & OPPORTUNITIES CHECKLIST

Remember: Goals + Opportunities = Success

GOALS

- [ ] *Craft Your "Elevator Speech"*
- [ ] *Create a Standout Business Card*
- [ ] *Design a Professional Website*
- [ ] *Blog on Your Area of Expertise*
- [ ] *Embrace Social Media*
- [ ] *Seek Out Live Presentations*
- [ ] *Develop Strategic Partners*
- [ ] *Join Networking Groups*
- [ ] *Create Your Own Networking Group*
- [ ] *Write Articles*
- [ ] *Write a Newsletter*
- [ ] *Advertise*

OPPORTUNITIES

_ *There are so many ways to promote your practice. Go through the list and see what marketing strategies you can commit to and are worth your time and resources.*

_ *In your closing letter to a client, mention that you are on Facebook, LinkedIn, etc., so that they can leave positive reviews.*

_ *In any blog, newsletter or article, provide your details and contact information about your practice.*

"SUCCESS DOESN'T GO TO YOU. YOU GO TO IT." – ANONYMOUS

CHAPTER 6

OTHER CONSIDERATIONS

DO YOU WANT A PARTNER?

As you launch your new firm, it can be very lonely. You should seriously consider if you want to partner up with another lawyer. There are benefits and drawbacks to both.

The benefits of having a partner are:

- **Support.** Starting and running your own firm can be a difficult, lonely experience without someone to talk to and share ideas. A partner can be a great sounding board and can offer differing viewpoints or ideas you may not have considered.

- **Backup.** A partner can serve as your backup if you are ill or on vacation.

- **Depth of Experience.** Aligning with another attorney can bring expertise that you may not have.

- **Larger Network.** A partner can widen your contacts and client base.

- **Complementary Strengths.** Each partner may have a talent for different tasks. One attorney may have strong organizational skills in running the firm and another attorney may be more comfortable in the "rainmaker" role of socializing and networking for business.

The drawbacks of having a partner could be:

- **Different Styles.** You might have a vastly different lawyering style than your partner. If you are one to dot the "i"s and cross the "t"s but your partner is more the "fly by the seat of your pants" temperament, there may be conflict.

- **Disagreements.** There may be disagreements in how you share the profits, run the practice, and work ethics.

- **Liability.** Under the Professional Rules of Conduct, you may be liable for the acts of your partner. You must implicitly trust any attorney you partner with and should share the same values on how to run a practice, handle clients, and follow the rules of professionalism, etc.

If you can't identify an "ideal" partner, don't worry. There are many ways you can collaborate with other attorneys without a formal partnership arrangement. You might share an office suite with other solo practitioners or network with attorneys in your practice area. You may enjoy running your own solo practice without having to constantly get consensus or agreement with a partner.

WHO IS YOUR BACKUP?

Especially if you are a solo practitioner, you will need to establish a backup attorney or network of attorneys who will be able to help you in case of an emergency or you have an extended absence. In most cases, professional liability insurance carriers ask for the name of your backup attorney.

Identify an attorney in your practice area that you trust and that practices law in the same style and manner as you do.

You should also consider who would handle your clients and cases if you decided to leave the practice of law. Planning for these contingencies will avert problems later and provide continuous service to your clients.

THREE RULES FOR A MOBILE LAW PRACTICE

While there is much flexibility to be enjoyed in a true mobile law practice, you should keep three rules in mind:

- **Be safe.** Many of our clients were people we were introduced to by someone we knew. Since there was a personal connection with someone we trusted, we felt comfortable going to those client's homes. And because we had each other as partners, we would agree to go to a stranger's house only if both of us could make the appointment. We would not have gone to a stranger's private home alone.

  If you do not have a partner and do not have a personal connection with the client, arrange to meet with the client in a public place. You can agree to meet in their office if they have one. You can meet at a coffee shop, library or community center. Many people live in communities with a shared event and meeting space available to the residents.

  Many lawyers you already know would be happy to lend you their conference room for an hour or two. We had a list of many attorney friends and business owners who allowed us to use their offices. Depending on our clients' location we would figure out the closest "satellite office" to them. Be sure to thank your friends with holiday treats or special gifts for the use of their office space.

- **Be prepared.** You should have your mobile office kit ready to go with your computer, printer/scanner, power cords. Notary book and stamp (if notarizing documents), extra pens and paper. If you are meeting a client at their office, try to budget some extra time after your appointment as they may want to introduce you to other potential clients.

  Also prepare your clients for what will be achieved at your appointment. Is it an initial consultation? A meeting to update them on a case or get their cooperation on a particular matter? A contract review or document signing? Giving a clear expectation of what you want to accomplish at a meeting will have it running more smoothly.

- **Be professional.** While it may be unconventional meeting someone at their home, you can still maintain a level of professionalism.

  Ask them to meet in an area away from distractions. Ask that any pets are secured or away from the meeting area to avoid distraction (unless, of course, the pet is comforting the client).

Dress as a professional. This rule isn't just limited to a mobile law practice. Just because you aren't working for a huge law firm and you are your own boss, doesn't mean you can be totally casual. You are your brand. What does your brand look like? You may not need a suit or tie, but dress appropriately and look sharp. People would like their lawyer to look like a lawyer.

TEN TIPS FOR A SUCCESSFUL PRACTICE

- **Set Expectations Upfront.** Be clear with your clients in how you would like them to communicate with you and how you will plan to handle their case. Do not "oversell" what you can do for them. Additionally, make sure they understand how and when they will pay you for your services so there is no misunderstanding later.

- **Respond to Clients Immediately.** One simple thing we did as attorneys was to return calls or emails the same day. We may not have had a complete answer at that time or may have just replied with a promise to get back to them at a certain time, but our clients were astonished that we were so responsive. Especially as you establish your practice, you can earn a reputation for proactive and personalized service by a quick response.

- **Don't Be Everything to Everyone.** You don't have to take every case. Say you are a real estate lawyer and someone wants you to probate the estate of a deceased relative. As hard as it is to turn down business, it may be the smartest thing to do if you are unfamiliar with that area of law. Spend time and effort on your practice area and become the expert there. Refer the probate case to an estate attorney. Typically, as you become more proficient in your area, the estate attorney you refer the probate matter to will be sending you all their real estate cases. Of course, if you wanted to get more experience in an unfamiliar practice area, you could co-counsel with another attorney and get their help. In all cases you consider, determine if handling the matter is worth your time and effort.

- **Don't Reinvent the Wheel.** There is much to manage with your own practice. There are many standard programs, procedures, forms, etc. to help you in your practice. Take the time to investigate what resources are out there so you don't have to do the work yourself. As we mentioned above, the State Bar Associations provide great information and resources for the solo practitioner.

- **Seek Help.** As you will never know everything about the law, you will never know everything there is to know about running a law practice. There will be times that you are stuck and may not have an answer. Constantly look for people who have the expertise you need and network with them.

  Find a "mentor" in your practice area. Don't worry that you might look "inexperienced" if you ask questions. Most lawyers were once in the same place you are in and many are happy to be mentors to you. Keep asking around until you find someone willing to step up. They can be of invaluable help to your practice.

- **Keep Networking and Marketing Yourself.** Even if your business gets busy enough for you, you should continue to do the things that brought that business in the first place. Keep a presence in your community, continue to speak in public, blog, and try to meet new referral sources. Connect with other attorneys on the web. And always carry around business cards! You never know who you will meet that might be looking for your services or knows someone who might. Do not be caught without your business cards as you might lose a marketing opportunity.

- **Set Your Goals and Stay Focused.** Set specific goals such as "I want to make $85,000 a year" or, "I want to draft contracts for XYZ client." You can't map out your plan or measure your success unless you know what goals you want to achieve. Write out your goals out with actionable steps to achieve these goals. The more you focus on your goals, the more likely you will succeed. Take the time to calculate the specifics of your goals. For example, if you want to make a certain amount, you must determine how many hours you must work and at what fee. If you want to get a certain client, you must plan how to get the attention of that client. Then, stick to this focused plan to achieve your goals.

- **Check Your Online Presence.** Google yourself. Enter your name and your firm's name into search engines. What shows up? Make sure you are aware and satisfied with your on-line profiles.

- **Be Flexible**. The one constant in any business startup is change. Be prepared to change plans, take advantage of an opportunity, or abandon a strategy that is not working. Try to identify what works best for your business and eliminate things that are dragging you down.

- **Keep Positive.** Starting your own venture has its ups and downs. Don't get discouraged in the beginning as it takes time to establish your practice and get a client base. Have a group of friends (they don't have to be lawyers) who you can talk to and who can encourage you through the difficult times. Remember the reasons why you are setting out to practice on your own. We started this book with a quote by Benjamin Franklin: "Energy and persistence conquer all things." Tape this quote to your laptop to give you encouragement during the difficult times.

HOW DO YOU QUANTIFY SUCCESS?

The grass is always greener... you may look at those attorneys in a large law firm and envy the steady paycheck, the stream of clients, and the job security. However, those attorneys are looking at your job flexibility, your autonomy over choosing clients, and your job satisfaction.

In launching a solo law practice, ask what truly is the worst that could happen?

What if you decided, after two years, it wasn't for you? You then could join with a firm bringing your entrepreneurial experience and client base with you which would be attractive to a potential employer.

What if you realize that you can handle part of the business but not all of it? You could join forces with another attorney who can bring a skill set that you need.

What if you couldn't make enough money to make it worth your time and effort? Then you could figure out ways to supplement your income perhaps connecting with other attorneys to help them with their case load, or becoming a legal plan services provider.

Michael F. Brennan, who wrote *Solo out of Law School* has a great perspective on failure: *"Think about failure. Picture the worst case scenario. What would things look like if you needed to admit that you didn't succeed as a solo attorney? Will your family leave you? Will you go broke with no hope of recovery, dooming yourself to life on the streets? Will your friends disown you because they can't imagine being surrounded by your negative energy? No, no, and no."*

Every attorney we have ever met had challenges in starting a solo practice and is continually challenged in their practice. Even the solo attorney who has an established practice has had his or her major setbacks. It is taking a huge leap of faith to go solo.

Working for someone else has challenges too: What if you were passed over for a promotion? What if the working demands are unreasonable? What if you hate being stuck in the office and can't interact with clients?

Determine what success means to you. Do you need a certain income to define your success or does success to you mean autonomy and job satisfaction? You may not be making the money you did in a large law firm but you have other advantages such as control over your time and destiny.

CONCLUSION

Starting and running your own practice can be extremely challenging and exhausting. It can also be professionally and personally rewarding. We hope this book gives you a headstart in planning and developing your practice. We encourage you to follow the checklists as you work through your goals and opportunities. Good luck going solo for success!

FOR MORE INSPIRATION, ADVICE & SUPPORT

Website: **www.gosoloforsuccess.com**

Facebook at **gosoloforsuccess**

Twitter at **@gosolo4success**

Instagram at **gosolo4success**

Pinterest at **gosoloforsuccess**

We hope you have enjoyed this book and found it useful for your practice. We know you are busy, but we would appreciate it if you would take the time to leave a positive review where you purchased the book and recommend our book to others.

Thank you.

ABOUT THE AUTHORS

Catherine Hodder, Esq. is an attorney licensed in Pennsylvania and Florida. Her experience ranged from managing financial and legal service companies to becoming President and General Counsel of a Business and Industrial Development Corporation.

Kelly C. Sturmthal, Esq. is an attorney licensed in Florida. Her background was in banking and worked for law firms focusing on Estate Planning, Real Estate, and Commercial Litigation.

Together Catherine and Kelly founded Sturmthal & Hodder, PA., a mobile law office, in Southern Florida. Their practice focused on Estate Planning and Business Planning. Their successful practice was featured in *The Palm Beach Post*.

While they enjoyed their law practice and working together, Catherine relocated to California. Kelly continues the mobile law practice and has founded a non-profit that promotes local businesses. Catherine writes about law firm practice management and estate planning issues. They both work together on www.GoSoloForSuccess.com to encourage and support solo practitioners and small law firms.

Made in the USA
Middletown, DE
24 November 2020